The Zechstein Sea

Patricia Farrell

The Zechstein Sea

Shearsman Books

First published in the United Kingdom in 2013 by
Shearsman Books
50 Westons Hill Drive
Emersons Green
BRISTOL
BS16 7DF

Shearsman Books Ltd Registered Office
30–31 St. James Place, Mangotsfield, Bristol BS16 9JB
(this address not for correspondence)

www.shearsman.com

ISBN 978-1-84861-263-1

Acknowledgements
Some of these poems have previously appeared in the following
publications: *AND*, *Stride* (online magazine), *Shearsman* magazine,
Shadowtrain (2007), *Greatworks* and the first *Other Room* anthology.
An excerpt from 'the Simultaneous Origin of the Fields of solvability'
was used by Bridget Penney for her contribution to the project,
The Responsive Subject. 'A.Life' was commissioned by Jivan Astfalck
for her installation series *be*twikst*.

The author would like to thank
the editors and artists for their support.

Contents

for Robert Sheppard

Straight

straight
and drained
and marked by paths
a slow game
at any time
stopped there
forgot to focus
ruins sheeted
hooves muffled

we make this picture
using only a cigar box
we can't see this
without it completing
in our minds
of the five legs
two of them are you

Practical Philosophy

take an animal into the house
an alligator or dog
say one of many different attitudes

above all
venerate your animal
with a necessary consideration
to its reasons

we need to think about the space
and orientation of this
our house

we need
to know
it is the diet
sufficiently
that makes it so
the existence
and habitude
of the animal

evidently

we make choices
but in the house the animal
begs space and freedom
long passages for the dog
long hours of sleep
for the alligator

do not sit upon
the aspirations of
this dog or alligator

The Tower of Silence (a-e)

a)

when the throat is cut
and the voice falls back
and on the floor
the things I see when I read aren't real
the cake shop
and right next door
the strange room in the cellar

he calls me 'little friend'
turning the flesh from inside out
and each time we died he wept

the earth floats
on the air
like a leaf
are the birds outside the window having fun?

b)

take the word *patient*
this has to be one thing
how can I understand
it also means another

performing the operation in my head
a notebook appears on the table
with four pencils beside it

c)

all this
a place arises founded on causation
a conjunction reason
that in the present case
either to suppose some beings exist
or that when the whole is in the whole
the absurdity of the two proves sufficiently
the supposition it resolves

ask me in thirty years and I will say

all this a place
arises founded on
causation a conjunction
reason that in the present case
either to suppose some
beings exist or
that when the whole is in the whole the absurdity of the two
proves sufficiently the supposition it resolves

ask me to walk past the yellow door
and I will say that this is not the same street

d)

common sense was wrong
salivating more for bread than meat

four pages of fine print
four hours of step-by-step procedure
two hundred stitches
sequentially from health to happiness
bathed and shaved
without a drop of blood
without a single scream

the pebbles placed on graves
make nothing in the mouth
ground to sand
we dribble to get rid of them

the prick of a pin
the pat of a hand
starting to say
more than you can prove
take one look at the brain
and throw it away in despair

sing

twenty-five sentimental songs
about breeding a non-viable food-source
which breaks its wings in zero gravity

e)

these three interests are related
the mouth waters
Little Friend

although they are decapitated
remember my enchantment
Little Friend

I learned how to sever
getting in from the outside world

listen to the electrical activity
listen through the telephone
Little Friend

I am nervous with behaviour
of leaving marks on the future
Little Friend

problems of life and mind
just roared with laughter as he does

we're provoking new lines of thought
cutaneous sensations
Little Friend

a will to simply intelligence
the material right juices
Little Friend

please believe
I do not exaggerate

falls straight through
and on the ground
Little Friend

the nearly perfect possible
excites me in the normal fashion
Little Friend

Snail Climbing

A line of men,
haphazardly across the field,
might be refigured
as nothing left to stand on.
Or would you retouch their eyes?

The same one is watching.
He inscribes "snail climbing"
as he walks across the floor,
going along with a concept
that all things are assembles
of smallers and of smallers,
all more or less alike.

What kind of day is this?
Here is all the weather of the world.
Is that Jesus?
He will tilt the globe a little
and maybe you will slide -
but you will not fall.
Do you understand?

The last dot contains
a compact version of the book of ages;
the law comes down
from the mountain or the mountain.

Whose Signature Is Hard to Decipher

let go of your handsome wings and flitter
waist-high to other men's failures

the chair to rest in is bathed in the light
of another dawn
I think me between those shores
one draped in the skin of another

the privacy of the living the dead and the only imagined

the failure of the first to play the game

he makes a clever landing
before the hands that drop him close
and then leaps down from the ground
letting the land rise up behind him
a victory though they kill him twice
his smiling head on seven sticks

we have postcards of all your seats of power

your domes to burn

anyone

even illiterates

could interchange these parts

shine you out serene
we will string you along
gambling with your fists

super-sharp you sit on nothing
backed by nothing
you can stare it out forever
the stage is always yours

sit you in a circle and burn your feet
cyan magenta yellow
bled by sunshine
wiped-out till only the rules remain

I crouch I catch I caress

once upon a time a place
few people many trees
(I the bombsight
I the bomb bay
I the release and everything else)

the intentional gaze
the empty banners
the sky so blue where no light reaches
on the line
a frame that will not fit

we are blue too
just pasted in
but now we have your number
to hide us from your curious eyes

the writing all along the road

is it up or down

the whole town turns inside its egg

in steady arcs

the coating on our eyes a comedy of errors

filter the ribbons that bind us

is this the place where the east ends

without windows

dying a presence more present than the quick

the flight from form that brings you down to earth

pick up the ball and run

first the smile and then the hinterland

your children's children

and their children's children

conjuring cinders and skulls

and bones in empty places

climbing fences to watch the centre fall

your regrets too late and backwards

coming to something beautiful

I stop there

to screw down my eyes

in a flood of light

from my little glass house

I see

one man stand inside another

do people lie

often

he who captures the land
will have lost the sky
all the craters filled with sunny lakes
the corpse is even smaller than the child
the houses smaller still

you sit in the lap of a dead man
his hand brushing your side
where there is no water
your formulas are obsolete

charm me in daylight and I'll fall in bits
along your chamber
condensing darkly into droplets
tiny but visible

we arise to star in our own deaths
keep you out and keep you in
with a wall of perfect bones
splice you right down to the helix

in total darkness

put common salt in water

through shuttered eyes

a bridge

I'll send you snapshots down from heaven

turn you night sky not seen by humans

the primary target is everywhere

already a master of begging
he'll hold his breath as long as it takes
while beneath your feet
his ponderous weight will twist the wrench

this is light eclipsed
tethered from inside the sky
you wish you too could fall

all a matter of force and
the law that determines
the attraction between two bodies
climbing till the sky turns black
do you have an art
to paint away our footsteps

go on I did not kill you quite

hang me just half-way

across your street

mask me

I'll sit there neatly blurred in death

where you walk on the floor

I walk on the ceiling

looking down on the pictures

of how I jumped from an artificial hill

and flew

my relation to the seraphs

a trick of light

igniting the combustion of each sleeping child

Blocks

Who would not love   if left easy,
and   everywhere?
Striking hard to loiter. What an effort,
when at the same time, you must say,
"I   like   everything".

The   behaviour   of   passing   faces,
a body   growing   continually,
and   beautiful now.
The skin of the world;   you
can't help but feel it   in your eyeball.

The   tragic   is   not   alien,
any more than   the   world   of   joy.
The word   "artefact"   does not make
a full day   that   everyone agrees:
a paper dropped,   a sound rolled.

Functionally   they   are   beautiful
and   it   all   adds   up
to   more   than apples
that   they   have   won,
more   than   two   heads:

in one   the formulas imagined   in
the other   a fantasy in symbolic logic.

The Same as Passion

light drops in sudden gushes
a diagram of
dense material aerial

this yellow
morning
may bear an object back
or bring it near
and blue
as indicative of distance

the threat of blue
is on the bubble's highest point

a foot slipped littered light
and drops in sudden phlegm

the fat dew of the ground

we are young gold
green
disorder made
cheerful and magnificent
white blossoms in the throat

synthetic days
dove grey
and this
can be remoulded
stumbled and left a smear
up on
the panting earth

the inside of an eggshell
measured by the eye
each separate leaf a torch

white on black produces blue

we
could think dissolving rays
to influence the brain
invading darkness at its trailing edge

the sun experiments with light
each green leaf red
a deal of green
chopped neatly into squares

a cupboard of blue fruit
with dust and ash and hair

an even tone
of cigarettes and paper

all of them
eventually
will be blue

from the window to the wall
all this
a kind of inky shadow

of back reflections from the grass
and glancing light
that shined against
the sunlight
bricks caked mud and flowers

the brown has dribbled from the white
paint that shit recalls

hair hangs out in space
the same heat as the stomach

between them
the only difference was white

the same as passion bears to light
disorder made fire-blue

Mr. Spinach, Formerly a Greengrocer, Until He Lost His Job, Takes a Walk in the Park

the ball is filled
with extraordinary gases
the valve released
and play begins

after five days
in the field
both man and ball
have shrunk

after nine
they begin to crumple
they struggle valiantly
to move

days later
ball tackles man
they
both collapse

Climbing

climbing on shoulders to view the street
the same now
retreating
but different then
hoisting him by his middle
watching beyond the waving hand
until after little years he slumps
then rises manifold
turned to the rejoicing
hiding something sweet behind himself
watching
crawling up the sides of his container
all joining hands
turning his way and that way
he sits so straight when the eye is upon him
falling backwards into his own arms
leading forwards and out

let us draw him in and put our hands together
swallow him on inspiration
hold our breath
and turn to face the eye in flight
we can look up at it and smile
look down
and inscribe his features on a piece of paper
grip the surface
and draw him with the wrong hand
then he will stare into space
and try to remember his next move
turn and we can rejoice in his memory
repeat it
an image of home

buttoned into our bodies
counting our hands and feet
we drift forwards
each other checking
for attempts to interlace our fingers
meeting ourselves
as we come the other way
and stop a moment
stop to watch the raising hand
stop to look away

bearing down on the back of his head
nothing changes after big years
we are still as small as we ever were
pulling at the lines on the blank surface
or as big but blinder
to the middle distance
passing the space from hand to hand
he has found a vantage point
leg raised to climb the next step up
nothing will stop us looking
wrapping ourselves around ourselves
and swinging forward and beyond
the same now
but arranged on different levels
bringing each other home
leading each other into the distance
a series of still moving bodies
along the street
looking over his shoulder

Yes, Things Were Down

Know boys are in another.
Girls' games could train hers before.
She pigs them brother!
Then asks.
Money pulls police, so stop nothing.

Sits red jelly open.
Can please, fine like ice.
Think, woe. Think, wow!
Lives.
Gives when? Gives how?
Sat black.
Works own icicle.

Thank head, ask her fast hand.
Went for; ran again.
Paint your water, which last tells right danger.
Going away, time flowers.
Friends must end if he, old, puts under with more station.

Here, blue birds by:
But trees makes farm.
Let's bring… a egg,
Apple…
I—No
My white road.
Our two snails.

Come, garden, take other room.
Pour like's afternoon plays long into chair.
Go and fell any from!
Got at big ones, me.

His not-day comes: would the will.
What little never left made talks that fly today.

This call toys.
It all wants, always;
Finds we be;
Draws name; says.
Said, 'place'.
Keeps up house.
Helps because I have some home.

First man was read.
Bad night gave back after reader.
Now you should next.
Clock sings as new;
Runs best. Had to.
Children, who found out about every good;
Don't see much of their round year.
Saw only morning.

Paperwork Enclosed

only everything's cool
don't bring selected skin
life's always top-side
tip contains next made

from number conscious levels
but you're just see
free to field customers
some why or gloves up

firstly eat this rub
whether have harder when
out mind lighten
hand pick in those ready

pack chance because indoors
spread split lines
do more leaks and put away
you've look longed small

above burden will perfect
available sets cooler lengthways
good hair helps
you can stack water

you can't stack steam
body leaves inside over
corner virgin is soon there
you'll abandon it during use

not change crumbled turns
ideas need full miss

load wrong find magic
how well locked lessons win

relax you'd get experts drive
easier spot says step it
bar fine cliff-edge
frank return matters

3 Pear-shaped Pieces

RADIOLOCATION AND THE DREAMERS OF LOVE
There are no definitive versions of the boats which wait to take us to the Island of Love. After the wars we developed ways of finding their origins on the Earth's surface, but the threat of aerial bombardment became serious. The public, decently girdled, demanded 'death rays'.

THE ART OF ABBREVIATION
In spite of military disasters and a crippling blockade we promised to pour paint into the waters to announce the contests of Duty and Love. The red-tinged bubbles burst and we were arrested (on political grounds).

LIFE, LIBERTY AND THE PURSUIT OF HAPPINESS
We would make our beds a litter upon the belly of this credo.

THE PERFECT WARRIORS
Whilst building the Dome of Sense and Soda-water, they were made uneasy by a certain conjunction of planets. Though small in stature, we escaped by twisting a rope of blankets, to discard our cares among the lilies.

POETS OF LOVE AND POVERTY
Shoulders humped we lament our silly age. Sometimes we feel ourselves hardly more than poets and not who we really are. To have robbed the police was the height of our address. Do you honestly believe that all that time we only talked philosophy? They were silly to look so far.

MELODRAMATIC RHETORICIANS OF THE SENSES
Our designs are geometrical. The armies parade the streets like gadflies. We will open the windows and be kissed.

FROM HORSE-PLOUGH TO ATOMIC PILE

Neither threats nor bribes will induce us. Ours is a spaniel's fidelity which will wipe the smiles from their faces. History always keeps a card up her sleeve. Drunk we fell from the boats and drowned.

A.Life

for Jivan Astfalck

Come little gentlemen
and tell us everything,
and make the cycle different.

This is not our planet any more:
this scrambled inventory that seeks the perfect square.
Just where the woman drops her parcels,
you can see the edge.

Take me for a natural
staring at a piece of glass.
Peering into stability,
in the path of totality,
we are removed and repainted.

If you think the circle
is forever a circle,
it is not.
Few things are certain,
but this is one,
we shall never live body to body at the same table,
no, not even in the same town.

This place used to be angelic
and no adjoining place has become angelic.

O there is a sad sort of clarity,
a strange fluttering
equipped with a handle,
if you can catch hold of it:
our eyes making the choice
from worlds overlapped like carpets.
Things become lively with the magic of use
flooding into this quiet hallucination.

With strict impartiality,
condemn every history that deviates;
the going out of existence of an angel
is that nothing goes out of existence.
We put on weight to keep out the cold,
and, on the third day,
the hay is mowed with a vengeance:
swinging from the gate,
head filled with grass.
Is life really as sad as that?

One war the victory will be mine.
But was it?
One hand daringly outstretched
beyond the three-dimensional world,
a bizarre confection of angel dust,
done without a horizon.
They would all curve
but they would not all draw the same picture.

I am a quite impossible bird.
True, its wings have been clipped.
I hop about bewildered
among my fellow men;
I never forget a name
I cannot quite remember a face;
everyone on the street is immemorial.
I am a jackdaw
who longs to disappear among the stones.

Think of us happy,
no membrane to bar our passage
and no virtue in hard work.
The world no longer looks
at you, as it should;
even this loose link is not impeccable.
I am matter and you are energy,
or else the opposite,
differently inflected versions of the same thing.
Or think of us as monsters of our reason.

We may yet live to say,
how much I wish I had the wings
that then I threw away.

I guess nature and time have changed.
In passing we unearthed it
but then covered it and forgot.
What will we see when we wake up?
The scale of the changes needed
will deter us
and we only keep it out
by a failure to invent it.
Though strange and charmed
and differently coloured,
there is not much to look at.

We could piece together
a civilisation in no time,
from within the collaboration of many nights;
we don't need to be aerodynamic,
each one a standing point
of the confluence of beams.

We verify the conditions
as we set new problems,
comporting ourselves
in the colours of necessities,
of new solutions,
new songs,
new misery,
so that you will not see
the stochastics of the Earth's corrosion.
At the edge of the sea does it occur to you all,
to the birds,
that these modifications
were never the base line
or a transforming of the integral devices?

Nature must begin to learn
there is an outside world,
cheer up if things start getting worse;
the way up and the way down
are both the same,
material soaked
to fix these passing fugitives' refraction.

Their grammar is too slow;
by questioning
you neither risk capture by
nor rescue the captives of
the pictures.

The troglodyte has his cave,
but you are practically suspended in mid-air.
The climate is strange
but I suspect you're used it,
staging but not staging
to profane the sacred space
and free the dimensions.

Now I am searching behind the mirror,
pecking at my own image,
ignorant of the nature of the heavens.
We don't smell our dead,
don't put them in the flames ourselves.
You are terrified of the approaching dawn
and I cannot sing;
what is the point of recalling this
our bestial life?
We have to judge
and may judge wrong.

As the toys come to life,
jewelled, whizzed and twittering,
we can lean together on this wind-blown world,
have pleasure in all things
or have pleasure in nothing.

The People's Applause
(after the German of Friedrich Hölderlin)

is it   not?
holy
my heart
full   of beautiful lives
and that
because I love

why damn me anymore?

in that
I am
wordful   and vacant?
masterful   and strange?

!

the multitude has fallen
that was so light-footed in the market place

and it honours only the arse of
we're all in this together

to the little gods
that you alone believe
they and you
are still the same

The Zechstein Sea

Describe a typical evolutionary event.

When was it?
Who was invited?
Who danced and who sat down?
What did you wear?
Who was in charge?
How was the atmosphere?

Describe your first journey alone

Let your ears tell the story
of how you heard the accidental misdemeanours
of all the boys and girls
who used the information
handed to them

only express this
if necessary
in historical sequence

during the little time/the time of tiny cherubs/ fat and thin
there lived /in the libraries and secluded courtyards
the fishes of our fathers /hanging inside the crevices
reading tales about themselves

this was the epoch /of peaceful angelic children
with voices like pealing chimes
one a sprite /with the innards /of a miniature piano
his neighbour /a late-flowering anchovy /living out
a laughing kindness

this was a warmth /so overwhelming /that both I and the fish
(of the time of the little ones) /ran back into the house /to cool off

ingress, outflow, reflux
the spontaneous generation of maggots
rill, runnel and freshet
life rising from the water
the father colours
and the mother colours
(two daughters, fourteen sons)
because we don't see
because we have eyes
we have eyes because we see

each morning
I cannot face up to
wearing my own skin
this might be the day
of the final calcinations
on which the babysitter
will carve on stones
for the later gods to see
my lasciviousness
and all my minor sins
and leave them
in the house.

think photonics
multi-layered reflectors
diffraction gratings
photonic factories
a brilliant blue mirror
see me; you love me
don't see me; you don't eat me

white limey oozes
their small chalky skeletons
fall down into the depths

think about nature
from a butterfly's point of view
and then think about
how to imitate it
copy the eyes and see

it is the 376th midday /of the dying year /and I am not
in a position /to tell you all the knowledge /that the scholars
would give birth to /because every morning /they will find
an excuse /not to tell /"we don't want to speak"/(?)
"we'd make waves, get caught and eaten"/(!)
"the children would /melodiously /never forgive us
and the music masters /who thank god are sleeping
would strut their stuff /and not give us any peace"

rumplecrumplederange
curlfrizzleandfrizz
cockle up, gather and frounce
as we age and crinkle

salt wit
biting, caustic, sharp
it eats itself, vomits and dies

the number of the beast
will deliver me safe conduct
by way
of dessication and embalmment
refrigeration, ensilage
canning and tinning

as the days get longer
and the years get shorter
the sea advances and recedes five times
each time our world is smaller
the load of salts and heavy metals bigger
and our backs begin to arch
against their natural line

------------------------- go into the sea
don't go --------------- into the mountains
------------------------- it's the same state in the countryside
------------------------- cross over the empty lagoons
keep going ------------ there is only movement

Gardening in No Man's Land

pink—if the demons
would have presented
they would not be black
they would be pink

open your mouth
and out pops a universe
always all ready here

place the bottle on the table
does space move
discreetly to one side
nudging
to the furthest reaches of the cosmos

or there is no bottle
only space
that ripples red in green

the soul weighs as much
as a slice of bread
we put the soul on the table
and shout at it

a figure right of vision
seeing it
as if
in the night sky
reading the avenues of trees behind it
and their shadows

what is
this beneath the stars

this is your journey
from Madeleine Street
to Autumndale Road
places which sound plausible
but do not exist

Pull out the plug; watch the water disappear down a thousand holes

this is

a device to get

off the hook just

for a little future

that needs to be done

cut

a tiger curled

against the door

what is the time

say not here

and the next thing

as above

is though cannot be

incarnate

saying

hooligans don't apologise

so below

to cut the grass

cut the grass

or cut the grass

turn up

side scrape

down from

the top of your head

that

proposition

cannot be

broken

a dependent animal

disciplined

split from mysteries

you are for

the chop

overneath and underhead

will gather leaves

if I remember

this is

the fight back

the bits

across the lawn

who's afraid

of the three dark mice

life's not

short

enough yet

not really here

simple

catch the beast count its legs

turn up the same

between different ears

at hand

the mountain

in the street

does it matter

just believe

and the dogs will follow

and believe

and they will lead

haul us back

onto the plural

just as it is

important to know

what side

your bread is buttered

a reader might be out there

in the landscape

perhaps that point

on the grass

possibly a leaf a fledgling or a turd

you might drop it

Issued a Directive to Paint it Yellow.
Why Yellow?

a tale of courtly love
a message baked into the porcelain of a coffee cup
                              either Greek or Turkish
before the café blows
revealing a series of emergent forms
                              2 to 2⅓ to 3 to 3⅜ dimensions
terrified by an accidental vehicle of near perfect linear perspective
the first death drawn from the engines out

excused service dives beneath a bridge
what space the space beneath a bridge
a Triumph Herald explodes
a Ford Anglia folds like silver paper
now every Saturday in black and white
the saloon car skids and crashes
the driver cannot speak to us
he can only smile and shrug

a grapefruit rolls from a bag of human remains
                              spiced and barbecued
not the grapefruit
a worm's eye view—a bird's eye view
a bulb not big enough to light the world
a lapse of time between frames

dismembered in a filing cabinet
this is an artwork
preserving even the shoes
I have made a meal for my family
I have made it in yellows reds and blues

Essays

(after Guillaume of Poitiers)

I

Friend
I will journey towards—make a verse—that (which) will
convince you

and it will be   (but hear me)

                      (solely) (from) madness

there is no sense there

and all of my and my and my cries
will be   of love and joy and youth

II

tenderly
tenaciously   indeed

and by a lively artifice
                                —which not even I can hear

or (only) a clamour in the willing heart/ (is the heart willing?)

the mind (and its stuff) cannot apprehend it

sorrow will leave us   sadly parting

                                if not to make a love

that finds   (invents)   its (brilliant) skills

III

Noble sir

your cavalier ways have played to my purpose:

        good and gentle
        good sound and adept/a gift to the militant

                         (be brave (my friend))

and no less able to take
measure

that each one of us can
not deceive the other
                         (without previous consent)

IV

If   fewer kisses

                    would tame my virtue

yes   no
vulgarity   (outside of everything)

                              in that case/at that time

fouling our garments
exhausting my stock of necessary things

how (what) better to conceal

                    the injury/the foolishness
                    of the living man

V

Despite the extremity of these revelations
            the depths of these mountains

                  most immediate/the moment of this moment

my (several) proficiency (my will of steel)
        makes strange

slowly/for a long time/languishing

It is your making
                  salvation
                        the protection of this edifice

VI

The other   touched (converted   cast)

nourishes this just place
(where) and each
                    no   look
how things look

this
          beautiful face

is to my knowledge

don't question   and don't acquiesce   or

I will make this little work
neither by sound nor by silver

VII

It is given

                by his   height above us
                by his situation

                to this peasant lord
                of the polite disputed landscape

(a splinter at the back of my eye)

        a gaze   a game of convenience

                  taking by way of covenant

what matters   if it takes a year

when (listen) tongue play makes sense like this

VIII

Sir give me the consolation of

                things not said (or known)

—that you may not be mad

                    flying

to insinuate the cause of them—

things do not tell me nothing
     (of quality)
            by their tenuousness (or touch)

neither of chastity
nor (deliberate) fire

IX

like a pair of iron bars placed close together

he holds the castle

                              as he is unhinged
                              living hand to mouth

and for the iconoclast
by his false (fated) step

he is obliged   most needful   the very man there
                              for(e) a stubborn foe and
                              marshall to all knowledge

two random numbers thrown together
give me   from either hand   his judgement

                  and let it fall
                  like rain
                  towards
                              the steady ground

The Simultaneous Origin
of the Fields of Solvability

a slow slide downwards
along a regular curve

it is summer very early morning
and that means nothing

all the yellows look cold
and so all the blues are warm

the solitary child gathers on the horizon
and moves backwards into the middle present

the past is a perfect (blue) parabola
but the future has been mended to prevent collapse

this is a model of always
what holds it up is invisible and to one side

maybe someone else can explain it

the blue car
a Ford Thunderbird

hits the bump and catapults
it is suspended in mid-air

the river remains in front
as the town remains to disappear behind

the child has gathered
all of created nature on his shirt

it was the bicycle that saved the world
doing wheelies on hard concrete to an ignoring public.

reading left to right we are going to end
either with or without an ice cream

he watches as his own car circles by

Homo noos the ghost man is coming from the mountains
announcing our becoming

in the early morning before we are awake
his feet fixed to his skis with parcel tape

the boy holds a fragment of the wall
he has punched a hole to look through

it is the right day and his face is smiling
decorated with cream eggs flour blood and dust

the silence has been digitally remastered
on the bus a Kekulé ring ignites one foot

it takes a committee to fail to second guess this structure
good Christian folks with a tube of glue

nobody chooses to write about this image

I am a system my name is Jiam Jayor
I will return your correspondence unread

a scrap of orange silk sellotaped to the lamp-post
look into the dragon's mouth

perhaps there is a dawn chorus of singing caterpillars
the sky is blue behind the picnic tables

maybe caterpillars sing all day
and perhaps you hadn't noticed

there is brightness just before the darkness falls
the walls are white the masks are white

the head has been torn off the man
who tried to hide behind a pillar

I do not wish to end on a rhyme or half-rhyme

The First Gun

the first gun
to feast here
settles its account

which in the living organism
gets down to the basics and vomits

weaker
and shorter in fibre

longing itself

not to subsist
in a banquet of haircloth

but in an above mere being
and essence of making do

this this expressly is
a sufficient quantity

and the tongue
a sufficient quantity itself

has tied
very small and unequal
a pulse

a radiating band
in the morass of modesties

and is put out
when modesties fade

into the custom
of only eating the flesh
of persons not of one's kin

inferior clothes
give no protection

mandate that
insofar as it is the eighth
(or ninth)
mark of condemnation

entangling
the names
'I know'
'to see'
'the end'

many sheets of paper
tired out
that insist together

in the manner of a material
on which the animals move and rest

The Outpost in Spring

two days before

the harbinger

a starling on a bridge

whose profile breaks the ice

a flat of hand

deals the covering card

the day before yesterday

bodying forth

in front of centre-stage

between the end-paper

and the fly-leaf